Hoppy the Second

My gran lives all alone
in a little cottage
at the end of our village street.

She is old,
and she forgets things,
but she is a very good cook.

Some Saturday afternoons
I get my bike out
and go down to visit her.

Sometimes she asks me
to do things for her,

and sometimes she asks me to stay to tea.

Then she bakes a cake, or cooks something special!

One Saturday last autumn I rode down to visit gran.

There was a white van parked outside her door.

Gran must have a visitor already, I thought to myself.

I left my bike outside, knocked at the kitchen door, and went in.

Gran was sitting down,
talking to a man in a white coat.
She looked very upset.
At first I thought
she was seeing the doctor,
but when the man turned round
I saw he was Mr. Parkinson,
the village vet.

I knew him, because he had been to see our cat once or twice.

"Hello, Mr. Parkinson.
Hello, gran," I said.
"Is anything the matter?"

There was a long silence.

"It's poor old Hoppy," the vet said at last. "He's not too well."

Hoppy was gran's pet canary. He was quite old too.

He had been in gran's cottage as long as I could remember.

I looked across at his cage. Hoppy was sitting on his perch with his eyes closed. He didn't look too good.

"You can make him well again," I said to Mr. Parkinson.

The vet looked away, and there was another long silence.

Then gran said quietly,
"Mr. Parkinson is going
to take him away
and try to do something for him.
But . . ."

She swallowed hard, and her eyes went shiny.

"I'm sorry, gran," I said. "Perhaps I'd better be going. I'll come down again next Saturday. I bet Hoppy will be well and home again by then."

But I was wrong. Hoppy never came back.

The months passed. I went to see gran more often now, to keep her company.

She missed her canary. Sometimes she would talk about Hoppy, and what a good little friend he had been.

Gran needed a pet to keep her company, I thought.

When our cat had kittens, I asked gran if she wanted one.

I told her she could have any kitten she liked.

But she didn't want a cat.

"It would scare the birds," she told me. "And I like to see birds eating crumbs on my lawn."

Then there was a puppy for sale in the paper, so I told gran about that.

"I couldn't afford to buy it,". she said. "I couldn't take it for long walks, and anyway, I'm not all that fond of dogs. Birds are the best pets."

"Then why don't you get another canary?" I asked her.

Gran shook her head.

"You don't understand, do you?" she said sadly.

"There could never be another Hoppy for me."

I was sorry that she didn't have another pet. She was so lonely on her own.

Then one Saturday afternoon I rode down to see gran with some eggs from my mother.

I had to ride very carefully with eggs in my saddlebag!

When I went into the kitchen, gran didn't say hello; she held up her hand and went "Shhhh!"

Then she pointed over to the window.

Sitting on the inside of the sill was a sparrow.

A fat cheeky sparrow!

I kept very still watching him.

The sparrow cocked his head on one side, and looked at us. Then he hopped across the sill and on to the cold water tap.

It was always dripping.

He looked all round, and suddenly he was upside down, having a sip of water.

He hopped back on to the sill,
and flew straight over
to the top of the gas stove.

He had his eye
on one of gran's tarts!

Cheeky thing, I thought.

Just as he perched
on the plate and began to peck,
I sneezed.

"Atishoo!"

The sparrow chirped in fright,
and flew straight
out of the window.

"What a pity. You scared him just as he was starting to eat," said gran.

"I've never seen a sparrow as tame as that," I said to her. "How long has he been coming into the kitchen?"

"Since that day last week when it tried to snow," gran replied. "He came in after crumbs, when I was asleep. Then when he saw I wouldn't hurt him, he got tamer and tamer."

"Now he's gone, I'd better shut the window," I said. "It's getting cold in here."

"It'll warm up when I start cooking," she told me.

"Leave one window open
just a little bit,
in case my sparrow comes back."

I left one window ajar
and shut the other.

Then I remembered the eggs
in my saddlebag. I fetched them.

"Thank you," gran said, and went on talking about this sparrow of hers.

I was glad to see her so happy again.

"But what am I going to call him?" she asked me.

I nearly said "Hoppy" but then I remembered what gran had told me about her canary.

I scratched my head.
"Don't know, gran," I replied.
"I've never heard of anyone
having a sparrow
as a pet before."

"He's good company for me
when I'm on my own," gran said.

That's fine, I thought.

"I'll think of a name,"
gran went on, looking round.
"But where did I put my glasses?"

"They're still on your nose," I said, trying not to smile.

"Oh how silly of me," gran chuckled. "I keep on forgetting things these days."

She went across to the table. "But I didn't forget that you were coming," she said with a smile.

"I'm making a special sponge cake for tea."

I grinned. I knew what gran's cakes were like!

"Now," gran went on, as she started to mix all the things together. "Would you do something for me while I make the cake?

"There's a letter that needs posting, over by the teapot."

I picked it up and turned it over.

"It needs a stamp," I said.

Gran sighed. "I knew there was something I had to buy yesterday," she said.

"If you take my purse you can buy a stamp."

"You'd better get me
a book of stamps as well,"
she added, as I went out.

I rode down
to the village post office,
bought a stamp,
and posted the letter.

Then I remembered the book of stamps.

I was just buying it when Alan Sanford came in.

"What are you doing this afternoon?" he asked.

"Having tea with gran," I told him, as I picked up the stamps.

We talked for a bit,
and then I said,
"I'd better go. Gran's cooking
a special sponge cake for me."
"Lucky thing!" laughed Alan.
He had heard about gran's cakes!
I got on my bike and rode back
as fast as I could.
I was beginning to feel hungry.

"You've been a long time," said gran when I walked into the kitchen.

"I saw Alan Sanford, and I stopped for a chat." I told her.

"Well, your cake may be burnt by now," she sighed. But I was looking at the table. The cake tin was still there!

Gran saw where I was looking and chuckled.

"Oh, how silly of me," she said. "My mind wasn't on what I was doing at all. I was thinking all the time about my friendly sparrow, and what I should call him."

She went over to the gas stove and opened the oven door.

"Matches?" I asked, handing her the box on top of the stove.

"All right, all right;
I know where they are," she said.
"I don't forget everything."

She lit the gas,
and shut the oven door.

"That should warm the room up a bit," she told me.

After a few minutes gran
opened the oven again.
"It's not getting very hot,"
she said, frowning.

"I wonder if it needs another fifty pence in the meter. Where's my purse?"

"I've got it," I said, and then I went very red in the face.

Talking to Alan, I'd left the purse on the post office counter!

How gran chuckled
when I told her.
"I'm not the only one
who forgets things, then,"
she laughed.

"Don't worry;
it'll still be there.
People are honest
in this village."

I rode flat out
back to the post office.

The purse was lying on
the counter, where I had left it.

Thank goodness for that,
I said to myself.

I raced back to the cottage.
"Here you are, gran," I panted,
"and there were three fifty pence
pieces in your change."

She looked in the purse, "So there were," she said, and gave one to me.

"One for you. One for the gas. One for tomorrow."

Gran can't really afford that, I thought, as she went off to the meter.

I put it back in her purse. She would never remember how much was there!

Gran came back and looked at the old clock in the corner.

"Your cake won't be ready for half an hour at least," she told me.

Then she smiled.

"But we'll have some of those eggs your mother sent me first. I'll do some special scrambled eggs for you."

She mixed up the eggs in a saucepan, and put them on the stove.

Then she cut some slices of bread, and put them under the grill.

"Wash your hands," she said, "while I make the toast."

I washed my hands, and turned round to get the towel.

I thought the stove was on fire! Clouds of black smoke were coming from it.

"The toast, gran!" I cried.

She pulled the toast out from under the grill, but it was too late.

The bread was burnt black!

"I'm trying to do too many things at once," said gran.

"Well, let me make the toast," I said, cutting some more bread. "Shall I open both windows and let this smell out?"

"Certainly not," gran said. She sniffed. "I like the smell of toast, and we want to keep the room warm, don't we?"

I like the smell of toast, too,
I thought, as I made some more.
But not burnt toast!

While I laid the table,
gran made a pot of tea.
Then she finished off
the scrambled eggs,
turned off the gas,
and we sat down to eat.

Gran pulled her chair close to the gas stove.

"It keeps my old bones warm," she said "Now eat up your scrambled eggs; your cake will be ready soon."

Gran's scrambled eggs were always very good, but she had given me rather a lot.

It was a bit of a struggle to finish what was on my plate.

We had a cup of tea,
and gran looked at the clock.
"Your cake won't be long now,"
she said.

I didn't like to tell her,
but somehow I wasn't hungry.

Not even for hot cake!

I must have eaten too much
scrambled egg, I thought.

I looked at gran's plate;
she hadn't finished
her scrambled egg, either.

She sighed. “I’ve a bit of a headache coming on,” she said, frowning.

“I don’t feel too good either,” I told her.

Gran said, “You’ve been eating too quickly, I expect. And I’ve eaten too much. Let’s just rest for a bit.”

She looked over at the window.

"If we keep still for a while, my sparrow may come back. Yesterday he hopped in looking for crumbs when I was having my tea."

We sat there quietly, and soon gran began to nod.

She often had a little rest after her tea.

I was getting sleepy as well. I wished I hadn't eaten so much so quickly, because now I was beginning to feel sick.

Suddenly I saw
the sparrow outside,
looking through the window.
He wanted to get in again!

He found the one I'd left ajar, and hopped through.

Then he perched on the tap, had a sip of water, and flew straight across to the plate rack above the gas stove.

He perched there a moment
with his head on one side,
looking down at the jam tarts.

Would he really dare
to start eating, I wondered.

One last look round
and there he was,
perched on the plate
and pecking away!

He really was cheeky.

As I sat there watching,
the smell of the burnt toast
seemed to make me feel worse.

My head was hurting,
and I felt a bit dizzy, too.
Gran really should have
the windows open, I thought.

The sparrow finished eating and hopped up on to the plate rack again.

He was scratching his head.

I was feeling much worse, and suddenly I thought of the eggs my mother had sent gran.

Were they all right? Gran wasn't feeling well, either, I thought. She had said that she had a headache.

I looked across at her;
she seemed very pale.

"How do you feel, Gran?"
I said. She stirred,
and mumbled something.

"Gran, I've got a bit
of a headache myself.
Perhaps those eggs
I brought you weren't too good."

She opened her eyes
and saw the sparrow
sitting on the plate rack.
He didn't seem to mind
the sound of our voices.

"Sparrow," she mumbled,
"Sparrow's come back.
Oh my poor head!"

She struggled to her feet
and held on to the stove.

"I'll get your cake out in a minute," she said, slowly. "Must have another cup of tea. Feel better then."

I said, "I don't think I want any cake, gran. I'm feeling awful."

"Must hot the water up again," gran mumbled, picking up the box of matches.

Her hand was quite near the sparrow, but he didn't move. He was getting really tame, I thought, rubbing my eyes. But then I saw that his beak was opening and shutting.

He didn't look at all well, either.

Had he eaten too much tart? I didn't like the look of gran.

I wondered if I should go and call a doctor. But then I thought we would look silly, if he said we'd just been eating too much.

Perhaps gran would feel better after another cup of tea.

My head was feeling very funny now, and I had to blink my eyes to keep them open.

Gran was propping herself up by the stove as she fumbled with the box of matches.

She wasn't much more than a metre away from the sparrow, but he just stayed there, opening and shutting his beak, as if he was gasping.

It was almost as if he needed air.

I sniffed. My head seemed to be going round and round, and now I could smell something else besides burnt toast.
Gas?

Gran was rubbing a match on the side of the box.

And the kitchen could be
full of gas!

"No!" I yelled,
"don't strike that match!"

I was too late;
the match scratched on the box.

But my voice scared the sparrow.

He fluttered into the air,
and then suddenly
he fell like a stone.

He hit the matchbox,
knocking it out of gran's hand.

Crumbs! That was close, I thought, thankfully.

I pulled myself to the windows and pushed them open. Then I opened the back door wide.

Fresh air rushed in, and after a minute or two my head stopped going round.

Gran was looking better, too.

"What's the matter with my sparrow?" she asked peering down at him. "And why have you opened the door and all the windows?"

"There must be a gas leak somewhere," I told her. "There's a funny smell in here, and I think it's gas."

Gran sniffed. “There’s no gas leak in here,” she mumbled. “I expect it’s the sponge cake you can smell.”

“Then what’s the matter with your sparrow?” I asked.

“Poor thing,” said gran. She bent down and picked him up. His little feet were sticking straight up in the air, and his eyes were shut.

Gran laid him gently down on one of her woollen gloves.

She frowned. "I wonder . . ." she began.

Then she half-opened the oven door. A hissing blast of gas rushed out!

She slammed the door shut and turned off the tap.

"The gas was full on," she gasped, "but it wasn't alight. It must have gone out while you were getting my purse, because there was no gas left."

"Then it came on again when you put another fifty pence in the meter," I added.

"We might have been blown to smithereens, if you'd lit that match!"

"Yes," gran agreed. She bent over the sparrow as he started to move a little.

"I think you're going to be all right," she said to him. "You just about saved our lives."

She picked up the sparrow and put him by the window in the fresh air.

Soon he was on his feet again, wondering what had happened.

Gran was smiling.

"Off you go, sparrow," she said.

But the sparrow chirped and hopped back along the sill. Then he hopped across to start on another tart.

He liked gran's cooking as much as I did!

"Well," gran was saying, "I've got a real little hero for a pet now, and I know what I'm going to call him."

"What?" I asked.

Gran watched the sparrow as he hopped about on the plate rack.

"Why, Hoppy the Second," she answered. "I know my canary would have liked *this* sparrow to be called Hoppy."

So these days gran has
Hoppy the Second
to keep her company.

He gets tamer every time
I visit her, and now he even
takes crumbs from her fingers.

Gran is the only person I know
who has managed to tame a sparrow.

But as my dad says,
she's a clever old bird herself!